MW00440132

THE
TRUTH DIVIDED

NAKIA JONES

BookVenture Publishing LLC
1000 Country Lane Ste 300
Ishpeming MI 49849
www.bookventure.com
Hotline: 1(877) 276-9751
Fax: 1(877) 864-1686

Ordering Information:
Quantity sales. Special discounts are available on quantity purchases by corporations, associations, and others. For details, contact the publisher at the address above.

Printed in the United States of America.

Library of Congress Control Number		2018940583
ISBN-13:	Softcover	978-1-64166-668-8
	Hardcover	978-1-64166-669-5
	Pdf	978-1-64166-670-1
	ePub	978-1-64166-671-8
	Kindle	978-1-64166-672-5

Rev. date: 04/25/2018

Acknowledgement

Editor Of Manuscript: Andrea Dardello

Editor Of Manuscript: Joseph Robertson

Graphic Designer For Book Cover: Lindsey Tufts

Photographer For Book Cover: Jocelyn Hurt Photos By J Photography

Dedication

First and foremost, I would like to thank Jesus Christ whom I owe all to. This book took a lot of blood sweat and many tears. President Barak Obama and Bishop Jakes I wanted to thank you both for allowing me a platform to help with bridging the gap between law enforcement and the community and it was an honor to meet you both.

I would first like to thank my Husband Kevin for standing beside me through this entire process and wiping my tears I love you so much, and to our children Phantasia, Kaila, Phalon, Jeremiah, Katherine and Kamryn you all are my reason for breathing as well as my reason for writing this book I pray as Martin Luther King said that one day you all will be judge by the content of your character and not the color of your skin or your gender. I would like to next thank my mother Jacqueline Green who has walked through this process with me and has been my encouragement when I wanted to call it quits, and to my dad Alvin Green who also encouraged me to keep going and never stop. Next, I would like to thank my friend Jocelyn Hurt she has been my rock this entire process and I adore you for that. I would also like to dedicate this book to my beautiful great grandmother Catherine, though you have gone on to heaven and received your wings I still feel your presence around me thank you for teaching me to stand.

Foreword

———◆●◆———

I power read from Thursday until late Friday night. All I can say is that this has the potential to be a film documentary as well as a published book. I was immediately drawn in to the different experiences personal, professional, curious to know what it was like as a black woman in the precincts. This book is necessary to be published, and I am confident it will sell more than what her expectations are. Can I just say "Thank you!" not only for allowing me to provide feedback, but I was deeply engaged in this story. After reading the entire manuscript, I was compelled to re watch the 2016 video and research this phenomenal woman even further.

Patricia Robinson

While reading the Truth Divided I relived all the hurt, pain, love, compassion, joy, anger, fear, and at the end peace. Because of God's grace, Nakia's unconditional love for her siblings and I, and a Twelve Step Program I am alive today. As the result of working Step Nine of the Twelve Steps I have been afforded the ability to make the amends that was needed to heal the hurt between us. Today I'm not only her mother but her friend, confidant, and biggest fan.

Jacqueline Harris'El Green

As a single mother raising a boy to be a man you face a challenge. But as a single African American mother raising a boy to be a man you face an even GREATER challenge. I have fears for my son, my ONLY son that a mother should not have beyond the usual fears. Will he leave and go to school and make it home safe because of the color of his skin, will he be judged or profiled on his outer appearance before you get to know him? These fears I have because of the recent police brutality against our young black males. When I read this book The Truth Divided it gave me a new found hope in our officers, one that had been broken and faded because of recent brutality against black males in our society. This book makes you see from another perspective one that you might not previously have thought about . It makes you analyze yourself and those around you. Are we staying WOKE? This is a great read for single mothers who like me have the same fears for our sons. It makes you aware and makes you think and gives you confidence in our Police Officers again.

Jocelyn Hurt

Introduction

On July 7, 2016, I would have never thought that a video of Alton Sterling being shot to death by police in Baton Rouge, Louisiana, would lead me to step outside of the thought process of my being a police officer and step into the absolute mindset of being a mother of two African-American males. I took off my blue uniform and replaced it with the civilian clothes that covered my brown skin. This duality would allow me to see myself as a police officer through the eyes of the African-American community. The rush of emotions pierced me like a sharp knife and I immediately felt hurt, anger, fear, and despair; the pain went through me as if I was being crucified. Then I began to think whether I would have to choose between the uniform and the color of my skin. As I took a deep breath and looked in the mirror, I searched deep within myself and asked, why can't I stand for both? Love, Unity, Honor and Respect have no color, nor do they wear a uniform."

As I looked in the mirror it seemed as if I had traded in the blue uniform that many people distrusted and disliked, for the color of my skin that so many people hate, although for different reasons. And it appears as if every African American has a bull's eye on their back. This injustice will only become removable—or obsolete—in that remote day in the future when prejudice, bigotry, and hatred might cease to exist.

Once I saw that disheartening video, I went to my private (friends-only) Facebook page and immediately posted a spontaneous video of my thoughts regarding my truth of this matter. Seeing the death of Alton Sterling vexed my spirit and made me question the integrity of the badge that millions of other police officers, including myself, wore every day of our working lives. I spoke of the hurt I was feeling concerning the total condemnation of all officers because of the actions of some bad ones, as well as the unjustified and senseless deaths of Black men and youth number of deaths caused by black-on-black crime, something I call a race destroying itself. How could I stand against the injustice brought on by my sisters and brothers in blue toward my race if I didn't address the fact that we are killing each other? I know many would argue that black-on-black crime and police mistreatment of African Americans are two different subjects and would wonder why I would be discussing them both in this book. My answer would be that I live both sides of this coin and they are both equally important to me.

When I speak on black-on-black crime I am pleading with the African American Community to stop destroying and killing one another so that we all can stand together as one unit, one body and have one voice when it comes to police injustice towards us. Why would anyone listen to us if we are our own worst enemy? As I've said many times before, a house divided against itself can't stand. I believe the quickest way to destroy a group of people is to do it from within because we know our own weakness and strengths. (WAKE UP)

I never would have thought I would be reliving the feelings of being so divided as those I had when the video of the Rodney King's beating splashed its ugly venom on the national and local news in March of 1991.

Some have asked why I have titled this book "The Truth Divided." I imagine that it is possible to see the truth from two different sides; if one looks at a situation through the eyes of another, the truth may seem very different from their perspective. What if one lives both sides of a divided argument? How clear would one's perception be? Then one realizes that somewhere in the middle is where the real truth resides.

Chapter 1

---◆●◆---

THE JOURNEY BEGINS

Many parts of my childhood were very hard and painfully unpleasant. When I think back on my childhood and recall the most painful experiences during that time of my life, I revisit the memories of my father being absent and enduring mental and physical abuse at the hands of someone I truly loved and who was supposed to truly love me. I always believed that I was my dad's little girl, and he was supposed to protect me from all harm. I remember during many times when I was being physically abused closing my eyes and saying, "I know my dad will be here soon to rescue me." My father not being in my life caused me to believe that there was no such a thing as a protector and in turn made me question if there was truly a God since we call him our father.

While the abuse continued, my dad never came. I was able to find a comforter and protector in my great grandmother. I remember the strength in her voice and her poise and the love I saw in her eyes.

When she looked at me I felt so safe. She person I was becoming. Throughout my early teen years, I watched my mother battle with drug abuse and addiction while trying to raise a family of five on welfare as a single parent. I became a teenage mother to my four siblings when my mom was unable to and took care of my mom when she was unable to take care of herself. On some occasions, I had to make sure my sisters and brothers ate dinner, completed their homework, and were prepared for school. There was a time when my mom came home so intoxicated that she threw up all over the floor and fell asleep in her vomit. I helped her up, got her cleaned up, and put her to bed so that my siblings did not see her in that state.

I remember going into her bedroom one evening she was lying so still. I started calling her name, but she wouldn't respond. I then started screaming her name and still no response. I believe my sisters and brothers could hear the fear in my voice so they came running into my mother's room. I quickly disregarded my fears to shield my siblings from what I thought was the death of our mother. They looked at me and asked me if our mother was okay. I immediately answered, she's fine. She was just very tired. Hurriedly, I took them into another room and got them into bed. I then rushed back into Mom's bedroom and called her name, but still there was no response. I felt fear and a rush of pain run through my body as I moved closer to shake her. After a few shakes, she woke up as if nothing was wrong. Tears immediately ran down my face. I hugged her and left out of her bedroom.

I had no idea how watching my mother battle with drug addiction was silently killing me. At age sixteen, I attempted to offer the ultimate sacrifice by trying to end my own life. After going through the ordeal of my mom not responding to me as I tried to wake her and believing she was dead, the thought of losing her became too much to bear. I thought about the look on my siblings' faces when they came into her room that day. I knew then I had to do something to save my family. I took two bottles of prescription pills that I had found in my mom's friend's bag and a bottle of aspirin. I believed that if I ended my life, my mother would be forced to see how bad her addiction to drugs had become and it would force her to get help. So that she would be a better mother for my sisters and brothers. I knew if I succeeded, the pain of losing me would be greater than the strength of her addiction.

It has been said by many that the closest thing to unconditional love is a mother's love for her child. On October 12, 1988 while lying in the emergency room bed after trying to kill myself with an overdose of pills, one of the doctors asked me why I had tried to hurt myself. I told him that my mom's drug addiction had gotten so out of hand and that I was afraid she was going to die and I figured if I died she would realize just how bad her drug problem had become and she would get her life together for herself and for the love and care that my sisters and brothers deserved. The doctor turned and looked at me with tears in his eyes and said, "No child should ever have to be put in a situation like this." He then quoted John 15:13: "Greater love has no man than this, that a man lay down his life for a friend," and as he walked out the room he said, "Young lady, I see greatness in you." The words touched my heart because they echoed those of my grandmother's. Before he closed the curtain, I asked him if I was going to die. He turned and said, "Not today."

Once released from the emergency room I was transported to Saint Vincent Charity Hospital (Cleveland) to undergo a psychological evaluation. Two doctors called my mom into the office where we were all sitting. The female doctor asked my mother, "Do you have any idea why your daughter would try to end her life?" My mom quickly responded "No." Then she said that maybe it was because of peer pressure. The doctor looked at her and said, "We have spoken to your daughter and she told us. I could tell you, but I think that she should." Fighting back tears, I looked my mom in her eyes and said, "I figured if I ended my life, it would make you see how bad your drug addiction had become and the loss of me would be so painful for you that you would seek help and stop using drugs to make a better life for you, my sisters, and brothers." At that very moment, I saw the love my mother had for me turn into a sea of tears. I had not seen my mom cry in years. Now, she tells me all the time that almost losing me was when she hit rock bottom. The next morning, she checked herself into a drug rehabilitation facility and has been clean from that day to the present. That makes twenty-eight years as of 2016. It is amazing how one person's selfless sacrifice can change the life of another--or the lives of many.

Part 1

——◆●◗——

NEW BEGINNINGS

After graduating from Shaw High School (East Cleveland, Ohio) in 1990, I was accepted to Wilberforce University (Ohio), the first college owned and operated by African Americans. There, I continued my education with the hope of becoming an attorney. The choice to become an attorney came from my love of the mock trial team that I was a part of while attending Shaw High School. Playing the role of an attorney, I believed I knew what my purpose would be in life. I always knew I wanted to be the voice for those who had no voice. Being a Prosecutor would also allow me to aid law enforcement to get criminals off the street. As an attorney, I would be in a position to get justice for those who couldn't help themselves, especially children and the elderly. This has always been my passion. I have also strived to be a good citizen and have worked hard to build a reputation as one who truly makes a difference in her community.

While attending Wilberforce University, I promised my great grandmother that I would fulfill her dream for me to become the first person in my immediate family to attend college, and I did. I chose Wilberforce because it was a small HBCU and it was not far from home. My best friend Cha Loe also attended with me. She always seemed to keep me on track. I felt pride as I watched so many intelligent African American men and women go above and beyond to reach their goals with such determination. No one was looking down on another. Everyone was helping each other move closer to reach his or her goals in life and the students pushed one another to their greatness. I learned the true meaning of brotherhood and sisterhood as I admired the sororities and fraternities.

Even though I admired them all I really desired to become a sister of the Alpha Kappa Alpha sorority but that is a dream that I have yet to accomplish. But God is not done with me yet. I was afforded to become a Kappa Sweet Heart, the little sisters to the fraternity, Kappa Alpha Psi. In my eyes, the Kappa's displayed the true meaning of what a real man should be. The Kappa's always dressed for success in their suits and ties, they spoke with dignity and respect and they treated us like little sisters they were always there when ever we needed them and to me that exemplifies the characteristics of a real man. The Kappa Sweet Hearts, an interest group that young women could become a part of until they are able to join a sorority, were made up of several different sororities. Seeing this taught me that though we may choose to go our different ways in life we are all sisters. The sisterhood and bonds that were created with my sweetheart sisters still exist today. YO SWEET!

I also admired the educators and staff. They went above and beyond to help students succeed. I remember getting phone calls in my dorm from some of my professors when I was not in class or my work was late. The funny thing is they could see straight through my excuses and made me accountable. I remember my professors saying I am here to help you succeed but you are responsible for your success. I am fortunate to have been able to attend an HBCU.

Chapter 2

---●---

THE BEGINNING OF THE DIVIDE

While attending Wilberforce a major event occurred that would alter the way I looked at the police. I remember it as if it was yesterday. The date was March 03, 1991. I turned on the news and watched as Rodney King was hit repeatedly by a group of white police officers with their night sticks. I began looking to see if he was fighting back, and he was not. On a few occasions he would try to get off the ground as officers struck him with their night sticks across his back, legs, and arms. The officers also kicked him in the head as well as stomped him in the head. After what seemed to be forever, the officers handcuffed King's hands behind his back and hog-tied his legs together. They then drug him off to the side of the highway where he laid face down in the dirt while the officers gathered together laughing and talking to one another with no regard to King's medical needs.

I immediately became angry and hurt at the same time because I could not believe that the police were beating a man who was not even fighting back. And to think they were the ones we depended upon when we need help. These were the people I looked up to. They were supposed to be the ones I could trust to protect me. I then began thinking: What had this man done to deserve a beating like this? Who is going to stop this from continuing? It seemed as if this video went on forever. The beating became so unbearable for me to watch that before I knew it, tears filled my eyes. They had beaten him so badly until I thought he was dead. I remember screaming at the TV, "They beat him down like a dog! Like an animal!" Rodney King did survive this encounter with police but sustained serious physical injuries. King described his injuries to include a shattered eye socket and a shattered jaw in which doctors had to replace with a metal plate. He also had fractured ribs and a broken leg as well as 1 other serious injuries. (2 Hudson Union Society published on May 11, 2012)

Many of my friends and family, as well as law enforcement officers I knew, began talking about the Rodney King encounter with the police. Some said that Mr. King was high off PCP2 (Phencyclidine or PCP a central nervous system depressant introduced as an anesthetic in the early 1950's but later abandoned because of unpredictable side effects such as agitation, disorientation, or hallucinations.) (3 MillerKeane Encyclopedia and Dictionary of Medicine, Nursing, and Allied Health, Seventh Edition. © 2003 by Saunders, an imprint of Elsevier, Inc. All rights reserved) and that the police had been fighting with him for a long period of time and what the video showed was officers finally getting control of him. I just kept thinking he was not posing a threat to the officers during the altercation, so why did they continue to beat him like that? I continued to hear people say he was high off PCP (this was proven false) and that is why Mr.

King was so out-of-control when the officers confronted him. I was still confused, having no idea what the effects of PCP were and still not believing that the police (my heroes) were just beating a man who was not fighting back.

Then the words that pierced my ears, as well as my heart, came from several people's mouths: "The police's response was racially motivated, it was said by many that he was beaten like that because he was a Black man." I remember feeling sick to my stomach and having a large lump in my throat thinking to myself that this cannot be true. The pledge to the flag that I had grown up with and was supposed to honor says "With liberty and justice for all." It did not say a specific race of people; it said for all. Then I began to think about whether I wanted to work on the side of the law that was going to discriminate against men and women who look like me. I became so divided inside, although I still trusted the judicial system. I believed if for some reason those officers had done something wrong, they would be found guilty. On April 29, 1992, the verdict was read in the case of the state of California vs Koon, Powell, Wind and Brise accused of assaulting Rodney King. The verdict was read, and all the police officers were acquitted of all charges, my heart sank, and I then watched as the riots erupted in Los Angeles.

I watched businesses being destroyed and police officers being attacked, but what really turned my stomach inside out was watching (Reginald Denny)3 a white male who was driving his truck to a delivery being torn from his vehicle by several Black males; they proceeded to beat him, kick him, and stomp him in the head. He was also hit in the head with a brick as if he was not a human being, in the same manner as Rodney King had been beaten. I remember yelling at the TV, telling them to stop stomping that man, since he had nothing to do with what had happened (neither the original beating nor the fresh verdict).

Becoming angry and hurt all over again, I wished to help Reginald Denny just as I wanted to help Rodney King. I asked myself why I felt so divided. I was so angry at the behavior of those police officers and just as angry at the Black males who beat Denny. But I later saw compassion has no color. Eventually, Denny was saved by T.J Murphy and his girlfriend, Terri Barnett, and her 8-year-old daughter, Mimi Barnett who were all African American. They took Denny to the hospital without regards to their own safety. There was said to be a fourth person who helped Denny, but their name was never mentioned. [i] The African-American community and the police all were pointing the finger. It was as if no one wanted to admit to the wrong they had done, and I understood the frustration of the African-American community because of the unfair verdict, but what I did not understand was why Reginald Denny, a mere passerby, was assaulted. The divide within me grew ever deeper and wider.

I started thinking about times in my childhood when I was judged by many because of the color of my skin: I was too light for some and not light enough for others. I hated the color of my skin, and many times I wished I could disappear. There was a time when I believed that my mother didn't love me because I was so light, so I took black shoe polish and tried to paint myself black. My peers would tease me and say in slave times I would have had it good because I would have been a "house nigga." I thought to myself that the "house

---

i   YouTube Report by Inside Edition reports on Reginald Denny rescue
     Published July 7 2012

niggas" had it worse. The Blacks that worked in the field hated them. They thought the "house niggas" had it better because they were so light and only lighter-skinned slaves were allowed to work inside the house. But in the house, the slave master and his family hated them even though they shared the same shade or pigment of skin color. To Master, they were still niggas. I believe that many African Americans still have that same thinking today. That kind of ignorant and destructive thinking will keep us divided. (WAKE UP)

Let me be clear about one thing before I continue: although I used the term "nigga" to emphasize my point, I despise the word and I never address myself or anyone in the African American race as such. I believe what a man speaks from his mouth becomes part of who he is and what others believe him to be.

Chapter 3

THE JOURNEY CONTINUES TO MY TRUE CALLING

My dream and goal of graduating from Wilberforce University and going on to Case Western Reserve for Law School was interrupted. I left Wilberforce University two years prior to completing my degree because my grandmother became ill, and I went home to support my mother as she and her sisters took on her care. Despite my efforts, I never returned. In May 1992, I gave birth to my first daughter. I realized then that I had to make some life-changing decisions as I was now responsible for not only myself, but for someone else who was dependent upon me. I decided a long time ago that welfare was not going to be an option for me. I did not want to be what others had said I would be: a single mother on welfare with several children. I was determined not to be a part of the system. I wanted better for my daughter and myself, so I became employed with the US Postal Service. The money was great, and I was afforded the opportunity to spoil my daughter while being a single parent and taking care of myself. I knew that working for the US Postal Service could be a great career, so I could not understand why my heart was not content. I felt I was supposed to be doing more. I could not drown out the sound of my great grandmother's voice saying, "I see greatness in you."

I began regretting that the two years I had spent at Wilberforce University studying pre-law was going to waste. My desire to help others was not being fulfilled and my purpose in life seemed to be withering away like a dying rose. I made up my mind I would not let a higher purpose of service in my life pass me by. So, after careful thought and prayer, I decided to apply to become a police officer. I knew I would be able to help others. My two years of pre-law experience could provide a solid base. I thought to myself that I would at last truly be in a career in which I could be proud and fulfill my purpose in life. After being an employee with the US Postal service for three years, I resigned to pursue a career in law enforcement, paying my own way through the Police Academy. I began training at the Cleveland Heights Police Academy in October 1996.

It was a journey I would never forget. During the first day at the Academy, I was very nervous. I knew I had given a lot of thought to pursuing a career as a police officer, but I could not help but second guess my decision. I kept saying to myself, I must have lost my mind; this is deadly serious. I could die out there. And then there were times when I thought, what if I have to kill someone? Maybe, I need to rethink this. But every day I kept coming back to the same answer: I wanted to make an important difference. The instructors at the academy treated us all the same, male or female, black or white. They wanted us to succeed. I remember many different trainings we had to go through and many different films we watched during training. But one film in particular played a big part in me making the final decision that law enforcement was my calling in life. I believe we all have a calling in life and there comes a time when you meet a crossroad in deciding if something is truly your calling. This film would be mine.

The film was about a female cashier in a convenience store that was being robbed by a male at gunpoint. Then, he just shot her for no reason. She was giving him the money with no hesitation, and he just pulled the trigger with no regard for her life. I saw her body fall behind the counter as he fled. I remember the country song playing inside the store as she laid helpless on the floor. I was so angry and frustrated; I kept thinking, is someone going to come and help her? Where were the police? Then I heard a sound I had never heard before: a long, slow gurgling sound. Tears filled my eyes as I asked my instructor what that awful sound was. He explained it was the cashier taking her last breath. She was drowning in her own blood. I went home that night and I could not shake the image of her lying there helpless on the floor, or the sound of that country song playing in the background. A week passed, and I still could not get the image and the sound of her taking her last breath out of my mind. It was so troubling to my spirit.

Finally, that week I walked into the Captain of the police academy's office trying to fight back tears and I asked if I could speak with him. He told me to have a seat and asked what was wrong. I explained to him that I initially believed that I would be a good police officer, but now I was having second thoughts about whether or not it was the job for me. I explained to him that I did not understand why I could not get rid of the image of the cashier being robbed and shot and just dying there with no help. I told him that I wondered what kind of police officer would be affected by a video, about something which I had no control over. The Captain then stopped me and said, "A great police officer."

He then said, "Nakia, your compassion for that lady tells me a lot about your character and because you wanted so badly to help her, and could not, it disturbed you; and that--that is the making of a great police officer." The Captain continued to say that police officers are the ones who run in to save others when others run out; they disregard their own safety to protect and assist others who need help. He went on to tell me that since I could not help her and truly wanted to, I felt helpless and that is why I could not get that image out of my head. He then told me always remember that I would not always be able to save everyone. The most important thing is to know I did my very best. If I allowed that rule of thumb to be my guiding principle, I would always be able to sleep at night. In that very moment, I knew I had found my true calling.

The schedule for classes was from 9 a.m. to 5 p.m., Monday through Friday and a few Saturdays and Sundays. While still maintaining a full-time job from 11pm to 7am as a security guard at a nearby hospital and raising my four-year-old daughter was very hard, I was determined to follow my destiny. The training at times could be overwhelming. We took so many notes that sometimes I thought my hands would fall off--and to think I had to learn it all to be prepared for the final test that I would have to take in six months' time. Our training consisted of, self-defense, tactical driving, and high-risk traffic stops, among other skills.

To my surprise, the most intense class of all for me was the shoot/don't shoot class with many different scenarios. In my mind, I believed this would be one of the easiest classes. I figured I would shoot the bad person with a weapon and save the good person. Simple. I believed I knew what a person who would do harm to me or others would look like but was I ever wrong. I got to experience without yet becoming an officer how officers had to make split-second decisions under an extreme amount of pressure, and how the wrong decision could change a life forever. The wrong choice in a shoot/don't shoot situation could cost that officer his or her life, or the lives of other officers--or, even worse, the lives of innocent bystanders or that of an unarmed suspect. One mistake could destroy the lives of many. And once a life is gone you cannot bring it back. Being a police officer is one of the very few professions I know of where if one makes a mistake in some decisions there is no such thing as a second chance.

It is strange how a person's own opinions of others can mislead their beliefs, for example, beliefs about how criminals are supposed to look. Opinions may come from what one was taught or the images seen on television. This can have a negative impact on one's interpretation of the facts. As a child, I thought all child molesters and rapists were white males because of television shows and listening to people who lived in my neighborhood. I also believed all gang members were black or Latino and this also came from misperception of television as well as what I heard and saw in my neighborhood. I also believed that women were more often innocent, and men were more likely to be a threat or a problem. I was in for a rude awakening as well as a cultural shock.

I remember that in my very first scenario at the Academy, I shot an unarmed black male who was merely going to the grocery store. My reaction was a result of my hidden biases and one-sided thought processes. I immediately assumed that he was the threat. I was sure that he was the person with the gun, but to my surprise it was a white female. That scenario alone made me examine my own prejudices and my one-sided thought processes. Had this been a real-life event I would have not only killed an innocent man, but I would also have likely been killed in the line of duty by the white female who I never suspected but was holding the gun.

I wondered how many others had similar thinking. I had no idea that I had such tunnel vision and limited focus about what I saw in front of me or what I thought my mind perceived; in short, I had prejudiced thinking because of my environment and I trusted others who I believed and in turn I adopted their beliefs (or biases). I think this is a straightforward yet powerful idea that all too often gets lost in a life without reflection. As human beings, everyone needs to reevaluate their thinking and judgment of others because of hidden biases, fears, intolerance, and bigotry. I thank God for the Police Academy: it helped me learn to look at the entire picture and then make an unprejudiced decision without making a judgment call because of a person's ethnic background or gender. The Academy also taught me to be aware of my conscious and unconscious stereotyping so that I might be able to make fair decisions to the best of my abilities.

Chapter 4

---•---

A HOUSE DIVIDED
AGAINST ITSELF

On September 22, 1996, I was sworn into the East Cleveland Police Department. East Cleveland is incorporated as a city but was originally established as a suburb of Cleveland. The ironic thing is this was the very city which had so dramatically changed my life in 1988 when I attempted to take my life and it began the new chapter in my mother's life when she became clean from drugs. She later became employed full-time in 1995 as an advocate for domestic violence victims and oversaw court-ordered management for perpetrators. In 2016, she retired as the director of the program. This was also the city where I had graduated high school. I stand in awe of the fact that I was hired by the city where some of the most important years of my life had taken place.

I was so excited being able to work in my own community and interact with the people who I knew personally. I thought to myself that I would be protecting my community from outsiders who would try to disrupt the law in the place I called home. I believed I would be capable of being a role model to little girls who looked like me and little boys who could be my sons. Life has a mysterious way of giving one a reality check when one least expects it. No one could have prepared me or told me that I would be protecting my community from itself; the very people that grew up and lived in this community would be the very ones I would be arresting. Many fellow officers who worked for the city said that if one can work in East Cleveland one could work anywhere. Because the city was so fast-paced, a police officer would probably answer more call in their first six months alone and be subjected to more situations than most police officers in any other suburb of Cleveland. I would soon find that to be true. The thing that I loved most about working for this department was that nearly 90 percent of the officers were like a family. We worked together without regard to race or ethnicity. We all had a tight bond. We might argue, curse each other out, or call each other out about our mess, but we officers held each other accountable.

As an officer in East Cleveland I interacted with the community on a regular basis. When I started as a rookie I was assigned to the Community-Oriented Police Unit, which helped me to get to know members of the neighborhood as well as allowed them to get to know me. My experience with community-based policing has made me a strong advocate for this type of law enforcement because it brings the community and the police together. I have always had a love for East Cleveland, but when an officer gets to know the community she is sworn to serve and protect, she becomes a part of that community just as they become a part of her.

The most heartbreaking part about working in a community I grew up in and had personal ties to was seeing crimes committed against people I had built relationships with, but what was even sadder was arresting those committing the crimes, knowing some were my neighbors or those I considered friends. I arrested many people I knew and some of them I arrested for some of the most unthinkable crimes imaginable.

I remember on one occasion a male walking into the police department asking if we had a warrant for his arrest. I kept looking at him because he looked so familiar. We checked our records, and nothing came up. A few minutes later an officer called out at Forest Hills Park and stated they had just recovered a female's body. As I looked closer at the male I realized he was my friend's boyfriend. When officers checked the body of the female, it was confirmed that this was my friend. The male in our lobby then confessed to officers that he had just killed her at his house in Cleveland and dumped her body in Forest Hills Park. It was unimaginable that this crime was done to someone who had lived in our community.

I couldn't believe that the same people who lived in the community with their families were terrorizing it and tearing it down brick by brick. I would go home from work on some days and ask myself, What's the purpose? I am arresting people who live in this community more often than not; how am I making a difference? I wanted to see change but the community that I loved and cared for was fighting against itself. That's when I realized what the Bible meant when it said, "And if a house be divided against itself, that house cannot stand" (Mark 3:25, KJV). I watched my city start to spiral downhill despite the people in the city who loved it and wanted it to survive.

I stayed with the department for three years and then moved on. East Cleveland is still fighting to stay afloat, but it will always be a part of my heart and foundation and that's where I learned to be the REAL POLICE! Before I left I remember going to a double homicide. I had never seen a dead body up close and I remember seeing a lot of my classmates and friends outside the store where these two young men's bodies lie inside a window. I felt myself looking at everyone around me crying and screaming and my heart just sank. I kept saying to myself, "They must be from East Cleveland."

Then I thought, "What if I know them?" One of the detectives asked me if I wanted to take a closer look at the crime scene. My heart said "No," but my curiosity as a police officer drew me closer and closer. That's when my world shattered. I saw my uncle grab a young man and say, "I can't believe that's my son in the window." It felt like a ton of bricks had fallen on top of me. Thankfully, as my knees started to buckle, and the tears started falling like a flood, someone told my partner that one of the men in the window was my cousin. My partner ran toward me and stopped me before I fell or even worse before I saw the body. The male that committed this crime was not only from the neighborhood, but he had gone to school with all of us. I believe after that incident I knew that I would not be able to complete my career in East Cleveland. It was too painful to watch my community destroy itself.

Chapter 5

——•——

CROSSROADS

After leaving East Cleveland Police Department I took a break from law enforcement. I was now pregnant with my second child and the doctors said it was a high-risk pregnancy. I decided to become a manager in a clothing store. On many occasions, I missed police work. I began to reminisce on a painful time in my life as an officer and how two officers' compassion towards me helped me through. I had only been on the force for about nine months and I found out that my daughter had been molested. It tore me to shreds. Anyone who knows me knows my children are my world. I couldn't believe that something so devastating could happen to me and my family. Because I was a police officer, I thought crime was not supposed to happen to me.

Watching a rape kit used on my four-year-old and making a police report left me feeling broken. This situation made me question myself as a mother. It felt as if someone was tearing my heart out of my chest. I can say this was one of the most humbling experiences of my life because it was the time in my life I knew I had no control. I got to sit on the other side. I got to feel what others felt. I stood in someone else's shoes as a victim of an unthinkable crime and not the hero. The two officers—an African American female and a White male--treated me with so much compassion and respect it was unbelievable. Both officers were very patient with my daughter and myself. The male officer left the room when it was time for the female officer to ask us very personal questions about the event. They both hugged me after they completed our questioning and the male officer kept reassuring my daughter that she was not to blame for the rape and that she was a very brave young lady to tell someone. They had no idea until later that I was also a police officer. (I commend those CP)

With a lot of counseling and a mother's unconditional love, my daughter was able to move forward with her life. As for me, on the other hand, it was a different story. The guilt I feel about the violation of my daughter's innocence I will carry in my heart forever. I felt like the one person I was supposed to protect over everything I had let down, and I was determined to never let that happen again.

About a year later while at work I had to interview a six-year-old girl who had been molested by her mother's boyfriend. I remembered how I felt when I was in that mother's position and how those officers treated me and my daughter. Not only was I able to show the compassion that the mother and daughter needed, but my partner and I obtained the evidence we needed so that the detectives could get a conviction of the perpetrator. The painful experience I had gone through with my daughter allowed me to help a mother and daughter through the toughest time in their lives. I truly believe if we were all able to look through the eyes of another or feel their pain we would be more compassionate.

I had decided that though I had experienced one of the most painful acts a mother could go through with her daughter, I wanted to have another girl. I believed I would be more than capable of protecting her from going through what her sister had gone through. I felt I was more equipped to raise a daughter than a son, especially since I was a single parent. I did not want a boy under any circumstances. I was so afraid of what would happen to my son as an African American male in this society because of crimes committed by black men against black men, especially if he did not have a positive male role model in his life, specifically, a father. I wondered if I had a son what kind of man would he become. I wondered if society would judge him because of the color of his skin and not, as Dr. King said, the "content of his character." I guess when you tell God your plans he laughs because a few months later I had a beautiful baby boy. I fell in love with him on sight. I had no idea that he would move me back into my destiny and change my life forever.

Chapter 6

YOU CAN'T RUN FROM
YOUR DESTINY

After the birth of my son, I went back into law enforcement. I went to work for Highland Hills Police Department, a small suburban municipality. I was back to my calling and in my heart, I knew it. I stayed with this department from 1999 until 2002. I always admired the Warrensville Heights Police Department. They were a lot busier than Highland Hills and with me still being young this smaller suburb was not busy enough for me. I wanted to do more with my career than just traffic enforcement. One of our officers had just left Highland Hills and was hired at Warrensville Heights. He called me one day and said that Warrensville Heights was giving a test and they had only one female officer. He then told me they were looking for more females. He also said if I was hired, I would make history as the first African American female officer hired by the city. I decided I had nothing to lose. The pay was almost triple what I was making. The city was much busier than Highland Hills, which meant I wouldn't get bored, so I took the test--the same test and hiring process that all male hires go through, including the physical agility test.

I was proud that I was able to compete with my male counterparts because the female officer who held the position before me was an emergency hire, which meant she did not have to take the test or go through everything all the males had to go through. Some of them talked about her like she was a second-class citizen; they felt as if she was handed the job and didn't have to work hard to get it. To my surprise, I scored higher than any other female who had taken the test that year. What I quickly learned is there was great responsibility, trials, tribulations, and pain I would have to endure with being the first African American female officer on the job.

Prior to me being hired, some of the officers were asking many questions about me. Some were very personal and had nothing to do with my capability to do the job. It was like some of them wanted me to fail before I was even given a chance. I often wondered if their response to me was because I was African American, a woman, or both. There were two officers who worked for Warrensville Heights that worked with me before. They were asked what kind of officer I was, and could I handle myself on the road. They both replied, "I would rather go into battle with Nakia than with most of the males in this department. "My hiring process was like a roller coaster ride. The questions from my polygraph test were extremely personal. I was asked about my sexual preference as well as other questions I regarded as private. Some of the answers were leaked throughout the police department. One of the officers who I was friends with was asked personal questions about me and was promised certain privileges if he revealed them. Despite the initial challenges, I was sworn in on Aug 6, 2002 as the first African American female officer for the city of Warrensville Heights. From the beginning, I had to be able to do the job just as well as or better than the males, even when it came to defending myself or my partner--and I did, I believe that some of my co-workers wanted a reason to say I couldn't do the job, but eventually, they saw that I could, so I earned their mutual respect. They learned I would never leave them behind, and I would go the extra mile to make sure we both made it home to our families. No matter how hard I worked to prove myself to many of the officers I worked with, there were some who would never respect me as a fellow officer. Their belief was that being a police officer is a man's job or at least they displayed that type of behavior. They did not believe that women should be a part of this profession despite the fact that women serve as Officers, Sergeants, Lieutenants and Chiefs.

Believe it or not, sometimes, my challenges came from not only the male officers but the other female officer who worked with me. There were times when my (Field Training Officer) had to go to his supervisor and inform him of how disrespectful she was behaving towards me, so he could tell her to knock it off with her smart remarks and her antagonizing behavior towards me. When she would be in our dispatching area she would, on many occasions, not answer me when I would call over the radio. She falsely told the other dispatchers that I had unlawfully run someone through LEADS, (Law Enforcement Assisted Diversion) which caused one of the dispatchers not to run people through LEADS at my request. I don't know whether it was jealousy or fear that we would be compared to one another. I could hardly wait until my probationary period was over, so I could give her a piece of my mind. But by the time my probationary period was over, she had begun treating me with the respect that I deserved. She offered her assistance to me when needed. She even asked for my help. After she left our department she and I talked. It was then that she revealed the hell she had gone through as the first female in the department at the hands of some of the male officers in our department.

As my trials and tribulation grew within Warrensville Heights Police Department, so did my love for the city and place I now called home. On many occasions, I was not treated with the same respect as my male counterparts by some supervisors. Derogatory remarks were made on more than a few occasions in regard to my pregnancies. On one occasion I was told by my supervisor that while on light duty due to my pregnancy I had to walk through the cell block to check on the prisoner. What was disturbing to me was that when the other female officer was pregnant, she was told by the same supervisor not to go into the cell block for the safety of herself and her child. On another occasion a different supervisor said in front of several officers once he found out about my pregnancy "Doesn't Nakia know how to use a condom?" In 2006, I was fired without cause and the city had to rehire me seven months later. Through it all, I have earned the respect of many from the community as well as some of my co-workers. The very things I thought would break me made me stronger. During my first few years working for the city of Warrensville Heights I noticed the job started to change drastically.

Unlike when I first started my career in 1996 or even when I began working for Warrensville Heights in 2002, I saw a drastic change in the communities we were now serving. Now, we were dealing with juveniles who had no respect for anyone, including their parents. It seemed like the black-on-black crime rate was rising. The children doing the killing were getting younger and younger. I could not believe we were taking real guns off children-I mean babies (eight-years old). And where were the parents? We started dealing with an overwhelming rate of people with mental disabilities and nowhere to take them. When I refer to people with mental disabilities, I am speaking of people who cannot care for themselves, people who need the correct medication in order to function in a normal capacity. Many of them would not take their medication and in turn they would end up on the streets. We deal with them day- in and day-out. What's so disheartening is the fact that we have nowhere to take them. The hospitals won't admit them unless they are a threat to themselves or others, and when we can get in touch with their families, they don't want anything to do with them. This becomes a safety concern for them as well as officers.

Another major change was the way the public viewed the police. The respect for the police seems to be obsolete. It appears that the only time the community liked the police is when they need us and even then, if we do not respond the way they want us to, they hated us. One time, I was assaulted by a 16-year-old girl who yelled at me, "I hate the police!" Then she yelled "Mike Brown bitch!" The most disturbing part of our encounter was that I was not initially called to the library for her. My partner and I were answering a call of a disturbance between two females, and she was not one of them. When I arrived and went to walk past her in order to speak to one of the females involved in the disturbance, she just started cursing and yelling, as if she wanted a confrontation with me. When I tried to deescalate her behavior by telling her to lower her voice in the library, she became even more irate. When I asked her to leave, she sat down and began making a scene. I then picked up her purse and told her she needed to leave. She refused. When I grabbed her arm to escort her out of the building, she pulled away and punched me in the face.

I was furious. Assaulting a police officer based on your anger about the confrontation that you heard about in the media is never justified. I have had people tell me they hate the police even though they have never had a bad encountered with a police officer in their lives. Few realize what our duties actually entail or the sacrifices that actually come with the job. They have no idea how many birthdays, Christmases, New Years, Thanksgivings, and special occasions police officers miss because of our horrible work schedules; how many times we neglect our families to make sure the families of the communities we serve are safe and happy.

Being a good police officer takes a selfless individual who is willing to work long hours for low pay (most receiving under $65,000 per year, according to the Bureau of Labor Statistics) and then risk his and her life for a community that has a love/hate relationship with them. Occasionally, someone will smile and say, "Thank you," and that is what keeps us going for the next several years. We are marriage counselors, parents to children we did not have, suicide preventers. We are the ones who notify families for some of the worst news imaginable. We are comforters, punching bags, and human shields. We are the ones people call when they can't call anyone else and we are the ones who come when no one else will. The truly good officers-I'm talking about the great officers--love their jobs and don't mind being all these things in order to save a life or to make someone's quality of life better.

Night shift for me is dreadful. I don't get to read my daughter's bedtime stories or laugh and talk with my sons about their day. I don't even get to cuddle with my husband. While my family is home I am out making sure the city we live in and our residents are safe. Once I do get home from work I am kissing my husband goodbye because he is on his way to serve and protect the city he works for--he is a police officer also. I then get my daughter ready for school and make sure my son is awake to drop her off at the bus stop. Before you know it, I am off to sleep for a few hours before my youngest daughter wakes me up for cereal and milk unless my mother-in-law is over; and then I can get some well-needed rest.

My children have no idea that Mommy may have just walked through hell to make it home. I always try my best to greet them with a smile and tell them how much I love them. My children give me the strength to keep going on days when I want to call it quits. My husband is my personal hero. He has watched me cry, scream, curse, and break down about situations I have encountered but who better to understand than someone who does the same job? While falling asleep, many times I think about the encounters, good and bad, I had that night and I pray for the people I encountered during my work day (especially the children and elderly). I thank God for every day I get to come home without having to take a life, and I thank God that my coworkers and I were able to make it home safely. After a few hours of unfulfilled daytime sleep, I am back at it again. I want to personally thank the good officers out there that risk their lives as well as thank the fallen officers who paid the ultimate sacrifice.

The public doesn't get to see the many sacrifices that officers make to keep their communities safe because that's not broadcasted across the media. Unfortunately, they only see what is presented in the media, and a lot of times, their hostility towards the police is based on a single story. For this reason, I have listened to many police officers say their love for the job has changed. They just want to make it home safely to their families and are afraid to go above and beyond for fear of being crucified by the media as well as the community. The tension between the community and the police is growing at an alarming rate, especially in the African American community. The videos of black males being shot by the police are going viral, as well as assaults on African American men and women by the police. At the same time, assaults on police officers, a well as their death, are being taped and applauded by many.

It used to be a time when getting up in the morning or evening to put on my uniform I knew I was going to save a life or make a difference. Now, I wonder if I am going to make it home or if my department will be sending a car to my house to tell my husband and children that my watch is officially over. The hate that the community has for the police is so hurtful for me because I know many police officers (Black, White, and Hispanic) who love their jobs and would gladly die in the line of duty if they had to in order to save a stranger. But I am not blinded by the fact that there are officers who disgrace the badge with their prejudiced beliefs and god-complex thinking.

Wearing this uniform is not looked at with respect any more. Instead, the police have become targets. And, at the same time, many African American men feel they are being targeted by the police. The only difference is they can't take off the color of their skin, but the police can hide behind their uniform. (I'M NOT SLEEPING)

Part 2

BLACK LIVES MATTER/ BLUE LIVES MATTER

Black Lives

Many people chant "Black Lives Matter!" without truly understanding where the term originated or what this organization stands for. The organization Black Lives Matter was started after the acquittal of George Zimmerman in the unarmed shooting death of African American teen Trayvon Martin. The organization was founded by Alicia Garza, Patrisse Cullors and Opal Tometi. They started the organization because they began to question how to respond to what they saw as the devaluation of black lives after Zimmerman's acquittal. [ii] This organization was not targeting the police. In fact, Zimmerman is not a police officer. The Black Lives Matter movement is very heartfelt and meaningful while others make

---

ii   Blacklivesmatter.com (Her Story)

no effort to understand its genesis or historical basis and so rally against it as subversive and violence-prone. Some say that when you make the statement "Black lives matter," you are disregarding other lives, but, in reality, those who use the phrase "Black lives matter" are actually empathizing with the loss of lives in the black community at the hand of the police and each other. That doesn't mean only black lives matter. I truly believe that this statement is saying, "Stop taking away black lives." It doesn't matter whether the perpetrators are the police or other blacks. The message is the same: Stop Killing Us!

What saddens me the most is that we have to say, "Black Lives Matter" as if no one else--even some in the black community-know that our lives matter. Why is it that we must remind ourselves and be a reminder to others that our lives matter? Those who get offended when they hear "Black Lives Matter" need a reality check. They should consider if they would be offended if their race was being killed by their own as well as the police and in some cases, unjustly by police. The statement "Black Lives Matter "is a way of saying, "We are hurting; we are crying out for help; we are angry; we are a part of the human race so why does it seem like we are being singled out?" I am African-American. My husband and children are African American. What makes another race more superior to us? My husband and I work hard to provide for our family. We are productive members of society. We should be treated with the same respect as any other human being and until we are, the statement "Black Lives Matter" will be necessary.

A Message to My African American Brothers and Sisters

Hey you! Yes, you over there chanting "Black Lives Matter!" Oh, I can see you're African American. You say you know and believe black lives matter. Well, I can't tell. "Why is it that I can't tell," you ask? Because you are killing one another! How can you agree with the statement, "Black Lives Matter ?" when you're killing men, women, and children who look just like you? How dare you say you have pride in your race but you disrespect one another and have so much hatred in your heart toward each other? Oh, yes, I know Black Lives Matter. And you say it matters to you young man Well, what about your black sons and daughters you left behind for their black mother to fend for alone? How do we show black lives matter by hating one another and being jealous of one another? How can we stand together as a race and say "Black Lives Matter" when our lives don't matter to each other? Once our lives truly matter to Us, then it will matter to others.

How can you stand and march with me and say, "Black Lives Matter" and argue and protest against police brutality knowing you would put a bullet in your brother's head over little or nothing? You would riot, burn, and tear up your communities and now your family has nowhere to shop and the small business owners in your community must go elsewhere. Do you really believe this is demonstrating Black Lives Matter? And demonstrate that we our Royalty I do know that Black Lives Matter just as you say you do but our actions are the true proof So I need for Us to make sure that we are demonstrating in not just our words but our actions that Black Lives Matter to us First! (I'M WOKE!)

Blue Lives

"Blue Lives Matter," (Originating in Dec 2014 Blue Lives Matter NYC was created to help law enforcement officers and their families during their times of need Sgt Joey Imperatrice and Office Chris Brinkley and Carlos Delgado compelled to show support for their brothers and sisters in blue and handed out bracelets that stated blue lives matter) [iii] Though many deviate from the original meaning of Blue Lives Matter and use it as a counter statement to "Black Lives Matter," when that was not what the organization was created for. Blue lives (meaning the police) does matter period. Blue lives consist of many races, so when I hear officers say, "I'm sick of hearing about Black Lives Matter," it implies that the lives of their fellow African American officers do not matter until they are in uniform. Police officers (Blue Lives) are supposed to be the elite who protect and uphold justice for all, without regard to wealth or race or gender. We protect and serve everyone. When the community sees the blue uniform, they should feel safe. We should never be the ones terrorizing the community because of our authority. To whom much is given much is required. I understand we are human and we make mistakes, but police officers who intentionally target people because of their gender, beliefs or race have no business in that uniform. So, take it off! These police officers have no right to chant "Blue Lives Matter!" These police officers are a disgrace to the badge and the greater community and are endangering the lives of those many police officers who do wear their uniform with honor and dignity. (OH YEA! I'M WOKE)

---

iii   Wikipedia Blue Lives Matter

Indeed, Blue lives do matter. I stand behind this statement. These lives consist of every race. The one common denominator is that we all get up in the morning, put on our uniforms, kiss our family's goodbye, not knowing if we will return. We protect our communities from people who would do it harm. We are the ones who run toward danger when others run away. We get low pay and horrible hours and sometimes the community we serve have no love or respect for us. What is happening to the human race. We are the ones who willingly lay down our lives for others. That's why Blue Lives Matter! Greater love has no man than this, that he lay down his life for a friend (John 15:13 KJV)--or many times, a stranger.

I have asked myself why such a division exists between black and blue lives. Most of us are fighting for the same things and if we just take off our hate and replace it with love and understanding, we would see that we are saying the same thing. If you ask a good police officer do they want to get rid of the bad ones, they would say "Absolutely! If you asked them why they don't stand up and speak out like Officer Nakia Jones did, I believe their answer would be something like this:

A Letter from a Great Officer

Why do you think I became a police officer? The answer is simple: So that I could be there to stop police brutality against you. I am behind the scenes making sure that this does not happen in my community while making a difference. I may not protest or publicly say anything, but I am watching out for you in more ways than one. I can promise you I will never allow another officer to mistreat you because of the color of your skin. Not on my watch! I will be that role model for your children, and I will make sure that you can sleep at night. I will uphold my oath to serve and protect, even if it means I have to protect you from my own sisters or brothers in blue. I am a good officer and I have no color. I just wear this uniform with humility and integrity and with the belief in justice and liberty for ALL.

Chapter 7

THE TRUTH DIVIDED

I always thought that my fears for my sons and daughters would be the career criminals on the street. I never thought for a minute that I would also have to fear for their safety when it came to the people who wore the same uniform as I do and took the same oath that I did. My children are very well-mannered, respectful of others, and they have been taught by my husband and me to conduct themselves respectfully when dealing with anyone in authority. But I was at a loss for words at first when my son, an honor student who graduated in the top ten percent of his class with a full scholarship to college, came home and said to me "Mommy, I watched a video circulating on YouTube of a man complying with the officer's orders, but he was still shot and killed by the officer." What do you say? How do I defend that? Now, please don't get me wrong. In some situations, deadly force is necessary. Many officers pray that we can complete our careers without taking a life. No person with a heart wants to take a life. We know that's the one thing we can't give back. As I stated earlier, anyone who knows me knows my children are my world and my son is my heart and though I love my job, and a few of the men that I work with are like brothers to me (black as well as white), it is my son who is my world and now I find myself concerned not only about his safety when it comes to the streets but also his encounters when it comes to my brother and sisters in blue.

On July 5, 2016, I would not fathom that one incident would make me step outside my uniform and show the heart of a mother. I asked myself was I in denial before or did it take the voice of my son to make me speak out for other mothers who felt the same fear as I did and to speak out for African Americans as well as Latinos who are being targeted because of the color of their skin. And what about officers like myself who risk their lives every day to serve and protect their community with dignity and respect? There have been officers shot and killed inside their patrol cars while eating lunch. Threats have been made against police officers and their families. These great officers are being targeted because of some disgraceful officers that shouldn't have on the badge in the first place. (THE TRUTH HURTS BUT IT HEALS)

On July 6, 2016, I arrived home that morning and did my normal routine; then off to bed I went. Later that afternoon I remember my son waking me up out of my sleep. I knew it had to be something important because everyone knows even the dogs don't wake me. I sat up deliriously and my son said, "Mommy did you see the shooting?" I asked him, "What?" Then I thought someone had gotten shot in our city or another young man had killed another young man. He then looked at me with fear in his eyes and said a police officer shot a man and killed him. The look in my son's eyes was that of fear and helplessness. I immediately sat up in the bed and he showed me the Alton Sterling video. While looking at the video I had my police mindset on. I immediately started thinking, what did he do? What was the call? Did he threaten the officers? Then, my son asked, "Mommy, is this going to happen to me?" I looked at my son and suddenly I saw the video through the eyes of a mother, sister, and wife of an African American male. I watched the video repeatedly and I could not fight back the tears.

I walked downstairs with my phone in hand and I watched it again. I felt a rush of emotions. I became angry, saddened, and frustrated. I could have dissected everything Alton Sterling did wrong, but then I would have to do the same for the officers. I would have to ask, "What did the officers do wrong?" The most crucial aspect of it all was another life of an African American man was gone. I looked at this video and screamed, "No! I'm so tired of this! I can't believe they shot him!" I watched two police officers yelling at a black male. Then one slammed him over a vehicle and pinned the side of his face to the ground. It looked as if the other officer was over him patting him down. Then I heard gun! and the other officer say, "You better not move!" Then shots rang out.

I was in shock. I kept thinking the officer shot him while his partner was still on top of Sterling, holding him down. I thought to myself, "What the hell?" Then, I heard two more shots as the officer rolled off Sterling. It was clear that Sterling was a big guy, but these two male police officers were not small. They were strong enough to wrestle him to the ground, but they couldn't keep him from getting to something inside his pocket that the officer believed to be a gun.

I know a situation like this can go from bad to worse but if that gun was inside Sterling's pocket and they had him pinned to the ground, he was not an immediate threat, unless he grabbed. I could not understand how two officers could not keep this male they already had on the ground from getting to this weapon without shooting him. Additionally, the officer that fired his weapon risked shooting his partner because of the way he was positioned on top of Sterling. I became sick to my stomach. I started to wonder if what the community was saying was true about us police officers. Are there some of us targeting African Americans because of their prejudices or fear? Was I being blinded by my uniform and badge because I knew I was a good cop and I knew so many other good cops that I couldn't see the few horrible ones right in front of my face? Was I starting to get tunnel vision again, trying to fool myself into believing that there was no racial issue between the police and African Americans? I couldn't believe I had just watched one of my brothers in blue murder a man and it appeared to be because he was black. Perhaps the officers were afraid of him because he didn't look like them.

Hurt and frustrated, I went on my private Facebook page to express my own opinion. I have had heated debates about police involved shootings as well as other topics related to the police on some occasions, my friends would get upset with me because I believe sometimes deadly force is necessary, despite the perpetrator's age. But, we always agree to disagree, and no one is ever disrespectful. I have sometimes had to explain to others a police officer's point-of view, and they were then able to see the situation from a different perspective and sometimes we would even find common ground. However, this police shooting shook me to my core.

After posting the video of my anger, hurt, frustration, and fear. I knew some of my family and friends were going to be shocked that I did not take up for the police, but I also knew that all of them would see how hurt I was and how torn I had become. I laid down for a few hours after posting the video on Facebook. I was awakened around 1:00 a.m. by my son. He then told me Philando Castile, another African-American male, was shot to death in front of his daughter and girlfriend by the police. He also told me that my Facebook video had gone viral. I asked him what he was talking about. That is when he told me the video had gotten over 1 million likes and that celebrities were tweeting me all over twitter and Officer Nakia Jones had become a hashtag. I went into his room and I saw that my personal video had shaken the nation. But how could that be? My Facebook page is private.

My son explained to me that my friends shared it; then their friends shared it and so on. I picked my phone up and went to my Facebook page. I had so many new friend requests and messages from people I did not know. The majority of them thanked me for speaking out and I just broke down and cried: reading how many people--Black, White, and Hispanic--were hurting was so overwhelming. The outpouring of love and support that I received was simply indescribable. At the same time, I had no idea that my world was about to be turned upside down and that some of the most unthinkable and hurting remarks would come from the people who wore the same uniform I wore. The next morning my home phone was ringing off the hook. My family called my cell phone screaming "You're on the radio." Soon afterwards, I received calls telling me that I was on the news "everywhere." One of the dispatchers from the police department called me and said, "Nikki, Girl, the media is all over city hall looking for you." I immediately thought, Oh my God. What have I done?

According to the dispatcher, the phones had been ringing off the hook, with people saying how much they loved me. And of course, there were those whose views were not so loving. When I was told I had to come into the police department and see the Chief, my heart fell to the floor. On my way in, I was told that some of the guys did not want to work with me anymore and that they were not going to back me on calls. I listened in disbelief. I was hurt. I had worked with many of these guys for fourteen years and I had always covered their backs; I had never left them in a crisis, so to hear the hate that was coming from their mouths because we had differences of opinions and knowing they could not respect my view as a mother just showed me who they truly were and how they truly felt about me. That is something I will never forget.

The meeting was a closed meeting consisting of the Chief, two others, and myself. I left the station in tears because I have a lot of respect for my Chief and the Mayor, so to see him so frustrated bothered me since I never meant for my opinion to cause so much stress for either of them. Our dispatch center was flooded with calls supporting me, although some did not. I began worrying about the safety of my family.

Many officers called to support me and to tell me that they were praying for me because they knew my journey ahead would be hard. The derogatory messages I received from a small number of people did not have an impact on me as much as some of the internal letters I received from officers. I received letters inside my mailbox at work that were so demeaning and disrespectful. Some of the letters had racial undertones. I had an officer send me a letter to tell me I was a disgrace to the uniform because I spoke out and I should be on welfare and go out in the streets and dance with the cooties (sic). For the next few nights I could not sleep. My nerves were shot as I went from Officer Jones to celebrity (which was never my intent). I did not think I could bear to see another African American male killed by the police unjustly; I did not want another good officer to be killed in the line of duty because of the actions of a few terrible cops; and I did not want to see another African-American male kill a child or another African American male.

When I thought it could not get any worse, on June 8, 2016, five Dallas police officers were killed while protecting the citizens who were protesting unjustified shootings of black males. Many wanted me to choose between the police or the African-American community and they wanted to know whether I supported Black Lives Matter or Blue Lives Matter. Some said, "If you are with the African American Community, then you should quit your job." I felt so divided: why should I have to choose since Truth knows no color. Why can't I weep for the death of Alton Sterling as well as the death of the five officers in Dallas? Did anyone see that lives were lost; that wives lost husbands, children lost fathers, mothers and fathers lost sons? What, precisely, is wrong with humanity? Why is one life more important than another one? There are good officers being targeted because of hate just as there are African–Americans, Latinos, and economically-deprived Whites being targeted because of hate. A large part of me just wished to turn in my badge and gun and walk away. But, deep inside I knew if one does not stand for something then one will fall for anything. Perhaps the change needed to start with me.

I was then asked on July 14, 2016 to be a part of a town hall meeting in Washington D.C. to help come up with ideas to bridge the gap between the African American community and the police. President Barack Obama was the host and ABC News provided network coverage. It was an amazing experience to be able to meet and speak with President Obama, but what I will remember most was meeting Alton Sterling's son, and his son's mother. When they embraced me, I broke down in tears. Sterling's son said to me "Thank you, Officer Jones. All I want is peace between officers and the African American community." I could hardly believe this was a young man whose father had just been killed by police. He was not filled with rage or anger. He just wanted peace.

I then had the pleasure of meeting a female officer from Canada who had lost her husband in the line of duty. She hugged me tightly and said, "We must bridge this gap for the good officers and the good community." I then knew it would only take a few selfless people to change the views and beliefs of many. I understood that the community needs the police but we also need the community. One bad apple does not spoil the bunch if the bunch is the majority, and I believe in my heart that there are only a few bad apples in the police departments and it is just time for the majority to say "Enough." If good officers and good citizens stand together then lives will be saved, but if we all stay divided, we will be a house divided that will fall. I wish we could all come together the way we did on September 11, 2001 and when I say all, I mean every member of the human race.

In the African American community, there are many of us who have worked hard to be productive members of society. Though many obstacles have been stacked against us, our determination to rise and be better has not been shaken. We are leaders in the community. We have established neighborhood watch programs to help protect the community when the police are not there. We respect our communities, and we support the good police officers. We want the police to protect us and get the criminals off the street so that we can sleep at night. We appreciate their sacrifice night and day to protect us. Not all African Americans pose a threat. I could be a young man on my way home from work trying to help my mom support our family, or a young man on my way home from college striving to make a better life for myself. I could be the next ER surgeon that will save the life of an officer who was injured in the line of duty. I am human, and the color of my skin should not be a death sentence, nor should the color of a policeman's uniform. I want to challenge community's leaders, pastors, police officers and the community to sit down with one another and listen to each other with an open mind and an open heart. I challenge you to trade places with one another and be open and honest with each other about your hurts and fears. Then begin to bridge the gap between the community and the police. We all must understand that we are all in this together and no matter how we try to divide the community and the police we need one another to truly matter.

The Epilogue

———— ● ————

STARTING TO BRIDGE THE GAP

Since the video went viral there have been many positive things that has happened as a result in many places all over the world. Communities and the police are working toward improving their relationships. Many people who once hated all police officers have changed their views of officers and have begun to judge officers by their individual actions. In one state, the Bloods and the Crips came together for a peaceful protest against police injustice. The last time this was done was in 1991 after the Rodney King verdict and I must add it was peaceful. I have been a part of many discussions to help continue to bridge the gap between the African American community and the police. I have appeared on the T.D. Jakes Show (America Beyond the Black and Blue) as well as BET who hosted Us or Else with TI. My son is now in his freshman year of college with a full scholarship, and I just celebrated my fifteenth year as the first and only African American female officer in my city. In 2018

I will be taking my first Gospel Play to the Playhouse Theater and who knows what else God has instore for me, as I continue a voice for those who feel as if they have none. I will also continue to wear this uniform with dignity, respect, humility, and love for all as well as let my actions and my voice be heard until the day when we all stand for Unity, Love, Truth and Honor in which none of these words have a color. (Stay Woke)

Letters

DEAR BLIMP/OFFICER JONES:

YOU MORE THAT LIKELY DO NOT HAVE THE GUTS TO READ THIS LETTER,
BUT PERHAPS YOU HAVE A FRIEND? THAT WILL READ IT TO YOU? YOU SHOULD BE ASHAMED OF YOURSELF!!
IF ANY OFFICER WHO ENDS UP ON T.V. RANTING AND RAVING LIKE YOU DID SHOULD NOT BE PERMITTED
TO WEAR A POLICE UNIFORM!!!!!! I AM A BLACK POLICE OFFICER IN AN ADJOINING DEPARTMENT TO
WARRENSVILLE HEIGHTS AND JUST SO YOU KNOW I AM A BLACK POLICE OFFICER AND NOT LIKE YOU, I WAS
PROUD TO BE BLACK AND WEAR A POLICE UNIFORM, BUT SINCE YOU DECIDED TO MAKE A FOOL OF
YOURSELF I AM NO LONGER PROUD!!!!! WHEN I OBSERVED YOU,MADE ME SICK!!!!! YOUR A JUDAS AND
A TRAITOR TO THE UNIFORM, WHICH YOU SHOULD GIVE UP AND GO ON WELFARE!!!!! YOU ARE NO
BETTER THAN A BLACK PROTESTER!!!!!!! I HAVE NOT SEEN YOU ON T.V. RANTING AND RAVING OVER
THE 11 POLICE OFFICERS WHO WERE SHOT IN DALLAS!!!! FOR YOU TO GO ON T.V. AND SCREAM AND YELL
OVER THE POLICE SHOOTING TWO BLACK BAD GUYS WHO HAD GUNS DISCUSSED ME. YOU KNOW NONE OF THE
FACTS, YOU WERE NOT PRESENT,YOU WOULD HAVE MORE THAT LIKELY RAN AWAY BECAUSE YOU ARE A
COWARD!!!!!! PLEASE KEEP IN MIND BEING ON A POLICE FREQUENCY AS W.H.P.D. IF IN THE VERY
GOOD EVENT YOU NEED HELP I WILL RESPOND NOT BECAUSE IT'S YOU,IT WILL BE BECAUSE YOU WEAR
A POLICE UNIFORM, AND FOR NO OTHER REASON.DO THE COMMUNITY OF WARRENSVILLE HEIGHTS AND YOUR
FELLOW OFFICERS AND HAND IN YOUR RESIGNATION!!!!! GO TO DALLAS AND DANCE WITH THE COOTIES
I SAW DANCING IN THE STREETS OVER THE SHOOTING AND KILLINGS OF ELEVEN POLICE OFFICERS!!!!!
AS YOU ARE THE WRONG SIDE OF THE FENCE!'!!!I HOPE YOUR CHIEF, BEING BLACK,FIRES YOU, YOUR
A DISGRASS TO THE UNIFORM. I AM THANKFUL THAT I DO NOT HAVE TO DEPEND ON YOU TO WATCH MY
BACK!!!!IF I WAS A POLICE OFFICER ON THE W.H.P.D. AND I WAS ASSIGNED TO WORK WITH YOU, I
WOULD CALL OFF SICK.YOU ARE A PERFECT EXAMPLE THAT CIVIL SERVICE LEAVES A LOT TO BE
DESIRED. YOU WITHOUT ANY DOUBT NEED MENTAL HELP, DO WHAT IS RIGHT, GO ON THE SICK LIST GET
HELP.YOU SURELY DID EAST CLEVELAND A BIG FAVOR. ONE QUESTION YOU SHOULD ASK YOURSELF, WHY
DID I QUIT THE E.C.P.D???? I WILL ANSWER THAT QUESTION FOR YOU. YOU WERE BEING THE COWARD
YOU ARE AND WERE AFRAID OF DEALING WITH THE COOTIES IN E.CLEVELAND AND CAME TO THE W.H.P.D.
E.CLEVELAND GAIN IS W.H.P.D. LOSS!!!! IN CLOSING,YOU SHOULD HANG YOUR HEAD IN SHAME AND GO
ON A DIET...CHANCES OF RUNNING INTO YOU ARE FAIR TO MIDDLEN AND IF SO I WILL TELL YOU TO
YOUR UGLY FACE HOW DISCUSSING YOU REALLY ARE!!!!!!!!THERE ARE THING ABOUT YOU THAT YOU
SHOULD BE CAREFUL,AS WITH YOUR ATTITUDE THEY WILL COME OUT. YOU ARE NO ANGEL!!!!!!!!

A BLACK OFFICER WHO <u>WAS</u> PROUD

OFFICER JONES,
HOPE YOU'RE PROUD OF
THE VIOLENCE YOU STOKED
IN DALLAS, THOSE OFFICERS
BLOOD IS AS MUCH ON
YOUR HANDS AS THE
SHOOTERS. YOU CAN
PROUDLY CARRY YOUR
NBPP CARD NOW.

PUBLISHED BY NOBLE, COLORADO SPRINGS, COLORADO

POST *Rembrant* CARD

OFFICER NAKIA JONES
C/O
WARRENSVILLE P.D.
4301 WARRENSVILLE CENTER RD
WARRENSVILLE HEIGHTS OH
44128

JIMI HENDRIX

July 7, 2016

Nakia Jones
Warrensville Police Department
4301 Warrensville Center Road
Warrensville Heights, OH 44128

Dear Nakia,

Thank you for sharing your powerful message about Alton Sterling's horrific death, the unjust deaths of other innocent lives, and the messed up legal system in our country. I have worked with police officers like you who have high integrity and are willing to risk their lives for others. I have also witnessed racism in action first hand by other officers. Your comments about both rang true for me.

I also heard your concern for your own children and the children in this country. Will they be safe? Another driver killed my son so I know what it means to lose a child through someone else's actions. Alton's parents, wife and children and extended family must be going through hell right now. The pain is all consuming. Unless someone has gone through that type of loss, they never really understand the depth and breadth of the agony for years to come.

More so than anything, I am grateful that you spoke the truth as a police officer, woman of color, mother, wife, sister, daughter, aunt, and community member. Our world needs more truth tellers like you. Be brave and hold fast to your convictions. They will carry you through hard times.

Bless you and your beloved family and may God keep you safe always.

With appreciation,

Jessalyn Nash

July 7, 2016

Dear Officer Jones,

I saw your Facebook video after the shooting of Alton Sterling. I know millions of people have seen it. I write to thank you for speaking out. You are a bridge that can help connect people. Without that connection there is only anger, ignorance, frustration and more dead people. I hope that you will not become discouraged. I hope you will continue to feel the way you do about your community and your job. I hope people will listen to you.

I do not pretend to understand your life circumstances. We live in different worlds. I am 61, Catholic, white and live in the suburbs between Baltimore, Maryland and Washington, D.C. What does connect us is a desire for people to respect one another, a desire

for justice in our communities
and all other communities; a
desire for all people to be safe
as they go through their daily
lives. You work in your community
to make a difference, and thank
God you do.

Last year I participated in
what is referred to as Citizens Police
Academy in my Community. This
consisted of 12 classes explaining
basic information taught to officers
during training, a 12 hour ride-along
with an officer, roll-playing of
what officers experience on real calls,
and some basic information regarding
mental illness and how officers
deal with it on the job. My
motivation to participate in this
was because a family member
was planning to become a police

officers. I knew nothing about the life, and knew no police officers. I wanted to understand more. Participating in this has made me more aware of everything related to the police. Yours is a difficult and important job. Thank you for doing it. Thank you for being a bridge between the police and the community. Thank you most of all for being a woman and a mother doing this job. You bring another perspective to a difficult and dangerous job — a very important perspective. Never feel alone out there on the job. Know at least that there is a 61 year old catholic white woman named Arlette who will be praying for you, your family, your community and our world.

Regarding the Alton Sterling shooting, thank you for expressing your rage and showing balance at the same time. Thank you for calling on those with prejudice and bigotry in their being to take off the uniform. They have no right to be doing your important work, and make it so much more dangerous for you and all other officers. Never be discouraged! Please continue to be that bridge. Every community needs people like you who want to make a difference. You will! You have.

Be safe and be strong,

Janelle B. Guest

Pictures

Mayor Richard Thomas @Ma... · 2m ˅

I commend Officer Nakia Jones for having a down to earth approach on community-police relations. Watch us on @BET tonight at 9pm @JonesNakia

♥ 11 likes

_jasminselena I was walking in the train and couldn't stop staring at this white rose. Everyone knows how much I love roses 🌹. My brother kindly bought it for me as an Early birthday gift . We walked our way to the BET Event Ti was Hosting to talk about Police Brutality. As we got a chance to hear amazing speeches that influenced us I couldn't help but be amazed by the wonderful Ms.jones . For many that don't know Ms.Jones is the police officer who made a video that went viral 8 Million views after seeing Alton Sterling Passed away . She stood up for us not against us, mother and kids waiting at home and knowing she'd take a bullet for any of us. We need more police officers like you Ms.Jones💕. I was happy enough to have been blessed to be able to say I was there today April 6,2017 to hear Your speech. As me and my brother both decided Ms.Jones deserved that rose , and there was no better feeling than getting up in front of everyone and Giving you a gift that will always stay with me, a memory , the best birthday Gift 💕🎂🙏. Godbless and thankyou . I didn't mean to make you cry lol thankyou for protecting our community 💕

21 MINUTES AGO

_jasminselena · Follow

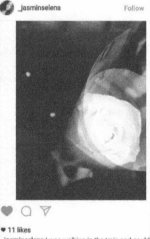

♥ 11 likes

_jasminselena I was walking in the train and could stop staring at this white rose. Everyone knows ho

WIN Network Detroit @WINNDetroit · 7/8/16
Morning #winnspiration from #OfficerNakiaJones. Make a
difference: be the positive change. youtu.be/6hBxxkgJCCQ

- NAKIA JONES, OFFICER

♡ 2

 GloriaSEA 🌀🌀🌀🌱 @NightShade10 · 7/7/16
#OfficerNakiaJones video
bit.ly/29xGQga on #AltonSterling EVERY LE & American
shld c! #BlackLivesMatter 👥

↻ 1   ♡ 1

 Media|Maven @VeronicaLKirk · 7/7/16
#OfficerNakiaJones Thank you so much for your honesty
and candor.

THANK YOU SO MUCH

Carbonated.TV @CarbonatedTV · 7/7/16

#OfficerNakiaJones Gives Fierce Wake Up Call To Officers Who Failed To Do What They Promised goo.gl/MekjHE

♡   ⟲   ♡   ⬆

Vanessa Clark @FoxxyGlamKitty · 7/7/16

Thank you, Officer Nakia Jones. THANK YOU. You've had enough and so do we.

#OfficerNakiaJones

♡   ⟲1   ♡6   ⬆

Remi Shop @RemiShop · 7/7/16

#OfficerNakiaJones ift.tt/29SjlZ4 Thank You Officer Nakia Jones #remishop

♡   ⟲   ♡1   ⬆

James Sarria @SustFoodStud · 7/7/16

Thank you #OfficerNakiaJones for your powerful words of wisdom youtu.be/6hBxxkgJCCQ #takeitoff

◯ ⇆ ♡1 ⬆

 FOX31 Denver KDVR ✓ @KDVR · 7/7/16

#OfficerNakiaJones shares powerful response to fatal shooting of #AltonSterling via.kdvr.com/lu8Hv

◯ ⇆38 ♡34 ⬆

Den Mother of Fandoms, Hater of Nazis @Rehfan · 9/15/16 ⌄
For those who have forgotten who #OfficerNakiaJones is:
here. Re-live the anger of a #GoodCop
#BlackLivesMatter 🐺

⭐Diva⭐ @ThisizDiva
I'm glad she spoke out! #AltonSterling #philandoCastile
#BlackLivesMatters #OfficerNakiaJones

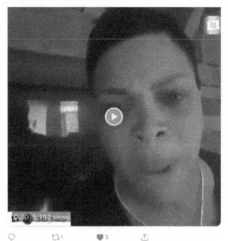

0:30 6,192 views

🗨   ⟲1   ♥3   ⬆

Shaun Pynne @ShaunPynne · 7/23/16
I'm so happy for **officernakiajones**
#ProudofMyHometownHero #officernakiajones
#OfficerNorman... instagram.com/p/BINUY5egbrr/

🗨   ⟲   ♡   ⬆

Las Maravillas @_lasmaravillas_ · 7/20/16
This week's #WCW goes to #OfficerNakiaJones. We hope
she inspires you to make a change.

#WCW Nakia Jones
lasmaravillassite.wordpress.com

🗨   ⟲   ♡1   ⬆

Natalia Rodriguez @NataliaRod96 · 7/20/16
This week's #WCW goes to #OfficerNakiaJones. Link in
the bio! instagram.com/p/BIGJCThA8Au/

🗨   ⟲   ♡   ⬆

QuestLyfe 🔫✊🔫 @QuestLyfe · 7/18/16
youtu.be/HHAIVHFrgWA #OfficerNakiaJones Some
people try to cut your legs off when you take a stand.
Thank you #KeepStanding. #WeNeedYou

🗨   ⟲   ♡1   ⬆

Joe braned @Thrilla_dondada · 7/16/16
Replying to @thegame
you help raise bread for that one cop but what about
#officerNakiaJones ?

🗨   ⟲   ♡   ⬆

William @He3Man7 · 7/15/16
@JonesNakia I admire your powerful deep stance. Giving
credit where due.
God/Jesus Bless 🙏🏆✝

Nakia Jones @JonesNakia · 7/14/16
Meeting President Obama.... Priceless. So humbled and
blessed by this experience #officernakiajones
#iamthatchange

◯ 5   ↻ 12   ♥ 32   ⬆

 Britt Fennell @ThisIsBrittneyF · 7/14/16
Would be nice to see #OfficerNakiaJones on
#POTUStownhall

◯   ↻   ♡ 1   ⬆

 Real Chi Youth @RealChiYouth · 7/14/16
We are about to try to contact #OfficerNakiaJones as well
in hopes to speak with her as well !! #whatsthesolution
#blacklivesmatter 🖤🖤

◯   ↻ 1   ♡ 1   ⬆

 Robyn Waunita Wright @waunita6 · 7/14/16
#officernakiajones #ohio #YESSS #democracynow
#tunein #kazifm "IF you are prejudiced as a law
enforcement officer... fb.me/7XEMxhmzN

◯   ↻   ♡   ⬆

 Moxiie @Naturalmoxiie · 7/9/16
We love and appreciate you #OfficerNakiaJones fb.me/
1I6x50yWt

◯   ↻   ♡   ⬆

 #DOAP™ #NerdGang @diaryofapoet · 7/9/16
#westheimer #Hillcroft 2 #goodcops #officernakiajones
this 4 U #AltonSterling #PhilandoCastile # #alllivesmatter

0:10 ·il. 26 views

◯ 1   ↻   ♡   ⬆

Alexandra Ionescu @Shuvitsa · 7/9/16
#OfficerNakiaJones is let's say the best

♡ ⟲ ♡ ⬆

Anita @im1rarebird · 7/9/16
"How Dare You!": Cop's Powerful Response to Deadly
Shooting of Alton Sterling #OfficerNakiaJones fb.me/
4haAcBFou

♡ ⟲ ♡ ⬆

AngelavandeWeerdhof @angiemoamedia · 7/9/16
facebook.com/nakiajonesprod...

Powerful Truth!!!! #MustWatch #officerNakiaJones

♡ ⟲ 13 ♡ 3 ⬆

Stephanie Matthews @StephM_Photo · 7/9/16
I'm just seeing this...it's had 8M views since being posted a
couple days ago. #OfficerNakiaJones broke it down...
fb.me/1jfInF5YI

♡ ⟲ 1 ♡ 2 ⬆

Nanny Goat @IrbyLena · 7/9/16
"How Dare You!": Cop's Powerful Response to Deadly
Shooting of Alton Sterling #OfficerNakiaJones
thegedsection.com/blogs/how-dare...

♡ 1 ⟲ ♡ 1 ⬆

Dear White Peepz @DearWhitePeepz · 7/9/16
"How Dare You!": Cop's Powerful Response To Deadly
Shooting Of #AltonSterling #OfficerNakiaJones
#BlackTwitter #BLM thegedsection.com/blogs/how-dare...

♡ ⟲ ♡ ⬆

Maan Ppl Mad At Black Panther Wakanda 💩 Is T... · 7/9/16
So a black cop voicing her opinion is treated worse than a
white cop who murders unarmed people 💩
#OfficerNakiaJones

♡ ⟲ 4 ♡ 8 ⬆

Ysa Adams @ysabellaw · 7/9/16
"Take that uniform off. You have no business here."
#Preach #OfficerNakiaJones Real Police.
#toprotectandserve Listen & learn #USA

♡ ⟲ ♡ ⬆

bishopjakes

#TDJakesShow

#Be that change

Alyshaa Jones
I remember about 2-3 years ago you arrested me for disorderly public conduct and public intoxication, she has been one of the most FAIR and respectful police officers I have ever encountered, and I've done some stupid crap growing up. I thank you for your service Officer Jones!! Not only did she make sure I was sober when telling me what I charged with, she really took the time to talk to me, like she knew me, treated me with the utmost respect. I will never forget the day you arrested me. Best day ever

Like · 👍141 · Reply · More ·

Agboola O. Olomola @agboolaolomola · 7/10/16

m.youtube.com/watch?v=_IOY2n...

#OfficerNakiaJones #droptheguns #blacklivematters
#whiteorblacksameblood #godblessamerica

 Kimli_ @kim_li · 7/8/16

#officerNakiaJones your video made me tear up
completely, your passion for mankind is so heartwarming.
Thank you.

> **Titus O'Neil** @ @TitusONeilWWE
>
> I'm sure #OfficerNakiaJones isn't the only Officer or
> Person that feels this way!I DO TOO
>
> Nakia Jones youtu.be/6hBxxkgJCCQ via @YouTube

 IG: @sharrieff__ @sharrieff__ · 7/8/16

BGLO singing voice: Calling all GOOD COPS to the floor, we
got #officernakiajones but WEthePeople need some more.
#altonsterling and others

 Luv LeSane @luvlesane · 7/8/16

#OfficerNakiaJones doing what we all should be doing, &
that is standing up for what's right & demanding justice,
Ofr. Jones I support you!

♡ 4

 Lynda Jones-Owings @mswedplanner · 7/8/16

"How Dare You!": Cop's Powerful Response to Deadly
Shooting of Alton Sterling #OfficerNakiaJones fb.me/
2hPv8VNcm

Amanda Rae @manndaraee · 7/8/16
Thank you #officernakiajones for finally speaking out for
the good cops out there against the bad ones 🖤
#blacklivesmatter🎤 #BlueLivesMatter

♡   ⟲   ♡   ⬆

John Coaxum @CoaxUpClose · 7/8/16
Praying especially for #OfficerNakiaJones tonight. We
have found a new leader/voice in the black community
heavy.com/news/2016/07/o...

♡   ⟲1   ♡   ⬆

RooperPMarshall @RooperPMarshall · 7/8/16
I'll say it again. #OfficerNakiaJones may not be the only
one that feels this way but she's damn sure the only one
who SAID anything!

♡   ⟲1   ♡1   ⬆

Bonny Rose MacDonald @BonnyTheWino · 7/8/16
Amen and thank you. #OfficerNakiaJones fb.me/IYFRTiyT

♡   ⟲   ♡   ⬆

Jenn @SweetieBird28 · 7/8/16
I couldn't watch the video that she was referring to, but
wow, everyone should take after her! #OfficerNakiaJones

antonio ✓ @antoniodelotero

#OfficerNakiaJones spoke out against police brutality -
she is the kind of officer every officer should strive to
be

David Braff @BaddaDanU · 7/8/16
For anyone unclear on what being a "good cop" means...
#OfficerNakiaJones is the benchmark.

♡   ⟲1   ♡1   ⬆

Chris Grasso @KingKameraman · 7/8/16
My father was a city cop so the events of the last few days
hit home strongly. Check out #OfficerNakiaJones FB
video, its powerful stuff.

♡   ⟲   ♡1   ⬆

😊😊😊DarkBastard😊😊😊 @DarkBastardNW · 7/8/16
regrann from my_real_truth - #officernakiajones
#restructure #thereshope #Regrann instagram.com/p/
BHnLHzQh1vw/

○ ⟲ ♡ ⬆

S'bu A. Mbambo @sbuM3 · 7/8/16
To #OfficerNakiaJones South Africa @presidencyZA
salutes your heroism...amandla! #Blacklivesmatter ✊🏿
@CNN

○ ⟲ ♡ ⬆

Toni Green @seedofcreativiT · 7/8/16
The fact that they're threatening to fire
#OfficerNakiaJones is sickening. A woman can't SPEAK
her peace but other can murder and still work

○ ⟲ ♡2 ⬆

shon hayes @shonhayes1 · 7/8/16
"How Dare You!": Cop's Powerful Response to Deadly
Shooting of Alton Sterling #OfficerNakiaJones
thegedsection.com/biogs/how-dare...

○ ⟲ ♡ ⬆

Ted Hicks @RealTedHicks · 7/8/16
Thank You #OfficerNakiaJones - you spoke from the
heart.

> 👀Quiet Observer👀 @BronwynJanse
> Black female police officer speaks out about the Alton
> Sterling shooting. She spoke with so much passion!

Sia Nyorkor ✔ @TVNewsLady · 7/8/16
.@SellersforMayor says #OfficerNakiaJones did not violate
#socialmedia policy cleveland19.com/story/32402834...
#AltonSterling

○ ⟲4 ♡8 ⬆

Sia Nyorkor ✔ @TVNewsLady · 7/8/16
Mayor: Warrensville officer did not violate social media
policy #OfficerNakiaJones #AltonSterling #SocialMedia
cleveland19.com/story/32402834...

○ ⟲1 ♡3 ⬆

🐾 Ill_Kalon Kakon_Ill 🐾 @IllOcherokeeIll · 7/8/16
facebook.com/hashtag/office...
#OfficerNakiaJones Lays it out!

○ ⟲ ♡ ⬆

Kelsey Knippschild ™ @iamtheewerewolf · 7/8/16
#officernakiajones is one of the greatest souls to stand up
in a blue uniform to the officers who murdered those men.
God bless her.

○ ⟲ ♡ ⬆

dina @dinajaye95 · 7/8/16
Other Police Officers need to speak out about police brutality&their fellow officers murdering people in cold blood like #OfficerNakiaJones

Q 2   ⇄   ♡   ⬆

KBthePT @sexeept · 7/8/16
#officernakiajones Girl, THANK YOU. #momtomom We need our people to hear you!!! #watchyourback now.

Q   ⇄   ♡ 4   ⬆

Noams @RosebuddNay · 7/8/16
'The most powerful, fearful, potent person in the world is an intelligent black man.' #OfficerNakiaJones

Q   ⇄   ♡ 1   ⬆

BizzyMomma @bizzymomma12 · 7/8/16
#OfficerNakiaJones - you are brave, you are strong, you are 100% correct & I salute you. #accountability

Q   ⇄   ♡ 1   ⬆

John G @jolomigri · 7/8/16
"How Dare You!": Cop's Powerful Response to Deadly Shooting of Alton Sterling #OfficerNakiaJones
thegedsection.com/blogs/how-dare...

Q   ⇄   ♡   ⬆

Michael 👻 👽 @michaelbroley · 7/8/16
Wow. #OfficerNakiaJones hits it on the head. Everyone should hear her. Everyone.

Q   ⇄ 1   ♡ 1   ⬆

Delgarno Newbold @lyndennewbold · 7/8/16
"How Dare You!": Cop's Powerful Response to Deadly Shooting of Alton Sterling #OfficerNakiaJones fb.me/ E4rClUf5

Q   ⇄   ♡   ⬆

Nancy Forde @nancyfordephoto · 7/8/16
#OfficerNakiaJones you have won my heart 2day and formed the words for so many broken hearts #hero #BlackLivesMatter ✊🏿

> Jamil Smith ✔ @JamilSmith
> Nakia Jones is an officer in the Cleveland neighborhood next to where I grew up. More cops need to be this pissed. pocket.co/sMhles

Q   ⇄   ♡   ⬆

Stephan(Steve) @Steve2016G · 7/8/16
"How Dare You!": Cop's Powerful Response to Deadly Shooting of Alton Sterling #OfficerNakiaJones
thegedsection.com/blogs/how-dare...

11:18 PM

Here's a picture of the event for you that illustrates how powerful it was. Thank you again!

You are my hero!!! 💯💯 You inspired in me the vision to reach out police as well as the community here. I was lucky enough to be asked to be part of a Black Lives Matter protest here in Omaha, NE that, thanks to the organizers, did just that. We had an estimated 1,000 people assemble so peacefully that both we, and the police, thanked one another publicly when it was over. And as I spoke to that crowd in the beginning about how to handle their encounter with police if they have one, I thought of you and how you'd want to be treated. THANK YOU for inspiring me!!!!! You helped us make a difference! ☺

Authors Biography

Nakia Jones is married to Kevin Jones who is also a police officer, they have 6 children. Nakia is also a well know Gospel Play write in Cleveland Ohio. Nakia believes with her gospel plays she can help restore hope and change lives one gospel play at a time. Nakia also goes out and educates the community as well as the youth on their rights and how they should conduct themselves when dealing with law enforcement. Nakia is considering writing a follow up book. Nakia wants to leave a positive mark on the world she believes that if you want change it starts with the person you look at every day in the mirror, she believes that if you want change you must be that change. Nakia Jones is the Female Officer whose compassion over the death of Alton Sterling shook the nation and she would never be the same again.

CPSIA information can be obtained
at www.ICGtesting.com
Printed in the USA
LVHW090726040919
629883LV00004B/1524/P